SUPER...DOPE...CHICK

SUPER...DOPE...CHICK

SHARHONDA L. SHARP

SLS Publishing, LLC

CONTENTS

I have told you these things so that in me you may have peace.
In this world, you will have trouble.
But take heart! I have overcome the world.
--- John 16:3 ---

__YOU__ are Dope as Fuck in real life!
I know it and you know it.
And now, so does everybody else.

Super Dope-isms

#QuoteMe
"My eyes are open wide.
Heart is feeling light.
Shoulders are no longer heavy.
I feel like I'm ready."

#QuoteMe
"As long as you keep treating Vulnerability
like a dirty word, you'll never experience
the true freedom it brings."

#QuoteMe
"Be very mindful of the people in your life
who always find it necessary to 'humble' you,
but never cheer you on."

Late Night Musings

<u>"Determine who you are, then be that ON PURPOSE!"</u>

The journey through and to Self is a long, hard one. There is nothing easy about digging deep to discover the whole of who you are and who you're actually supposed to be versus all that shit you previously thought.

From birth until the point when we've decided we've had enough, we are shaped by those closest to us and the experiences we've had. So many outside influences impact our decisions when we decide on our identity. Most of those early stages are just a lot of mimicking and mirroring of others around us or things and behaviors we think we "should" be like. Those early years are mostly just trial and error on a constant loop...because rarely do we really learn the first time.

The harsh, detrimental life lessons usually come on the heels of something we are certain will destroy us. After multiple bouts of that, eventually we get tired and actively decide we never want to feel that way again, or give outside influences that level of access to us. We begin to iron out life goals and dreams. We find more positive role models, mentors and idols to look up to and learn how to accomplish those goals we set.

We take a more active role in our own lives to construct it the way we want. The biggest FLEX is taking ownership of Self. Self-love, Self-esteem, Self-awareness, all those things. It's about YOU! It's been about YOU! The minute you accept that is the first of many steps, you'll take on this endless journey of Self-discovery.

The layers you'll shed. The baggage you'll unload. The tears you'll cry. The shackles you'll loosen yourself from. It is all worth it. The journey to Self is one of growth and growth requires discomfort. You have outgrown certain areas of your life and your discomfort is proof of that. It's time to move past it. It's slowing up your progress. Let's go!

A Queen by Another Name

S-H-A-R-H-O-N-D-A
Sha-Rhon-da
Capital "S" with a capital "R"
right in the middle for a lil' flavor.
Sha-Rhon-da

Annunciation is key and required when you address me
My name is an artistic homage to my ancestors
A collective collaboration creatively coupled together
My mother channeled the powers of God & Thought
Meditated and marinated maternally for months
Put some respect on my moniker!

Sha-Rhon-da
The "Sha" is for Sheree with a twist
Invoking the influence of my Prima Artist
The "Rhonda" stands alone, needing no further explanation
Much like the Queen who boasts proudly
about me carrying her name
In honor of Strength, Serenity and Self-sufficiency,
I bear a name that is the combination
of two beautiful Black Queens

My name comes with a legacy and rights
to a Queendom attached to it
My name makes pulses race, hearts skip beats
and draws the highest level of attention

My name inspires curiosity
It is the leadoff to interesting conversations
Influencing insights immediately

The name, itself, is common culturally
Spellings, expressions and purposes come verily
But none of them are Me
My name is my own and I'm selfish about mine
There is an obligation that comes with the privilege of knowing me
Put some respect on my name!

My name requires the full use of your tongue
and conscious correction
The use of nicknames is a hard-worked for grace
that is not awarded freely
My name is ShaRhonda
You may address me as such
No, you may not call me anything other than that
Because I don't fool with you like that!

The life I've lived has been done so on purpose
I am the stubborn sole-survivor of a shit-drenched past
I've broken nails and sweats to dig myself up and out
Trauma Trenches, Hills of Heartbreak and Dirt Roads of Drama
have been clawed through to get here
And you think I will allow myself to suffer
the indignity of such simplistic shortenings by strangers
because you can't read?!

S-H-A-R-H-O-N-D-A
Sha-Rhon-da
Nine glorious letters arranged like a beautiful symphony
Bach, Mozart and Chopin could never compete
Divinely designed and dutifully dedicated to me

Read it
Learn it
Speak it
Know it
But DO NOT take liberties with my shit!

My name is Sha-Rhon-da
For good measure, I'll say it twice.
Sha-Rhon-da
But if you must call me anything else,
QUEEN will suffice.

For Rhonda ♥

Hellion

There's a special place in Hell for women like me
Seated at the right hand of the Devil
Just to annoy him with our audacity
To smile and smirk with sweet suspicion
Toil away the days going against the grain
That is our afterlife's mission

There's a special place in Hell for women like me
Those of us who laugh in the face of danger
Welcoming it with open arms and gritted teeth
We cradle adversity to our bosom like a precious babe
Singing holy hymns and lyrical lullabies in outrageous octaves

There's a special place in Hell for women like me
Warrior Women built for battle
Ageless Angels who soar without wings
Quintessential Queens reigning without apology
Thick-thighed, thorns in the side of Satan on a Thursday

We are the Phoenixes who rise from ash and soot
We fan the flames just to watch them dance
We are the rage and the calm that ignites infinitely
We are the Children of the Cinders,
leaving coal-laced footprints in the sand as we carry the world

We are iron and metal that is molded and resurrected,
yet still heat resistant
We are the pleasure derived from the pain

We are the long-lost treasure with immeasurable value

Oh, yes!
There is a special place in Hell for women like me

Women who refuse to be silenced
Women who defy death
Women who turn nothing into EVERYTHING
There is a special place in Hell for women like me
We are the voice in the ear of the enemy
when he thinks he has you

Not today, Satan.
Not today!

War Cry

Babygirl, love yourself enough to know you deserve better
Know that it ain't just about sustaining through stormy weather.

Babygirl, honor yourself enough to not stay where you're triggered
Know that whatever dream you have, you need to go BIGGER

Babygirl, have the Audacity to demand what you deserve
Know that your joy is limitless in this world

Never put the responsibility of your happiness
on the shoulders of someone else.
Never allow yourself to play it safe and settle for less.

Babygirl, the world is yours
If you keep letting others clip your wings, you'll never soar.
Babygirl, dance in the moonlight and smile at the sunrise.
With every passing day, your soul has lived a lifetime.

Infinite and omnipotent
Glorious and excellent
Perfectly imperfect
A delicate package
Built to withstand but handled with care in the right hands.

Babygirl, my heart beats and bleeds for you
Knowing there's so much you've endured
I need you to know you're so much more
than what you're judged for

Bruises, contusion and blissful illusions
Cocktailed with harmful recreational uses
Babygirl, you're more than this
Whether you know it or not, you da shit!

I applaud you
I salute you
I stand with you and for you

Babygirl, I love you
I just need you to love you
Because when you do
You are un-fucking-stoppable
And I love that for you.

Lake by Oshün

Rise above...

Stretch forth your hands...
Cradle the sun in your bosom...
Hold the world in your womb...
Kiss the moon goodnight...
Place the stars in your crown like diamonds...
Breathe the essence of existence effortlessly...

Brush your fingers against the ocean...
Chisel and etch your name into every mountain...
Dance in the dirt, enchanting the buds beneath...
Smile with your eyes...
Cry with your song...

Pearls of endless wisdom...
Petal-soft touches...
Divine destiny dictating your diction...
God pledging his devotion to YOU...

The Spirit of Shango is calmed by you...
The Epitome of Ecstasy and Evolution...
Spinning pulsars...
Timeless galaxies...

Waves crashing due to an over-swelling of emotion...
All of life created by your hands...

Rise above, My Queen.
Rise above...

For Loni ♥

Super Dope-isms

#QuoteMe
"See me for who I am and who I am becoming,
not for who I used to be or who you wish me to be."

#QuoteMe
"I may not be perfect,
but I'm perfect for MY PURPOSE."

#QuoteMe
"In the midst of the madness
is where you grow the most."

The Harmony of a Haiku #1

Life is a cocktail
A shot of pain
A splash of pleasure
An olive of hope
And God stirs it all up

Super...Dope...Chick

Soooo...I'm Dope as Shit!
And I meant that as arrogantly as it sounded
It's ridiculous how Dope I am
Should legit be illegal
Matta'fact, it probably is...

Well, lock me up and throw away the key
Place me in Gen-Pop on Cell Block C
Let me walk amongst my revelers
as they admire my strut in shackles

Let them bask in my glow that refuses to be dimmed
under these dull fluorescents
Let the guards push and shove their way to me
Just to be gifted the opportunity to escort me
The pleasure will be all theirs, I'm so sure

I'm Dope as Shit!
Unapologetically so
Oh, I tried keeping it secret
Didn't think the world was ready for the likes of me
But Mama says, "If you stay ready, you ain't gotta get ready."
So, buckle up, Cupcakes! Because this train is moving

Barreling down the tracks at full speed
Carrying a heavy load and you don't wanna miss it
The power in my engine drives and delivers more power
than them lil' petty horses under your hood could EVER!

Your lil' putt-putt could NEVER!
Boxcars of beauty, brains and bodacious audacity
ticking along these tracks of life
Stopping traffic and making hella noise at the same time
Do not challenge or play "Chicken" with this luscious locomotive
Just sit still, be humble and wait your turn
But be patient because I'll be here for a while

I'm Dope as Shit!
And rightfully so!
I've earned this!
I've worked hard for this!
I've been through some shit!

I was built for this!
I was made for this!
I asked for this!
I prayed for this!
I'm Dope as Shit!

You know why?
Because I am pure

I allow myself to feel and be felt
To cleanse and be cleansed
To love and be loved
To cry and be laid open
I embrace the most vulnerable sides of myself
Because they are the best parts of me

I'm Dope as Shit!

Because I'm Dynamic...

I'm a Jackie-of-all-trades
and what I can't do, I can fake my way through
I feed souls who lack the nourishment they need to be great
I water the seeds of ideas I plant in the minds of others

I ensure they never forget me
I put my heart in all that I do because I know
that even the most minute task is apart of my greater purpose
I...AM...DOPE...AS...SHIT!!

I mean it
I believe it
I see it
I own it
I don't apologize for it
And I invite you to witness it
I...AM...DOPE...AS...SHIT!!

Because I am Me...
There are no carbon copies or clones
What I'm made of cannot be duplicated,
only appreciated

To get close to this Dopeness is a grace
not awarded and afforded to many
And I'm not slowing down anytime soon
So, get a good look and make it quick

You DO NOT want to miss this
Because I am one Super Dope Chick!

Weapon of Choice

My pen is mightier
than any weapon formed against me
My God and My pen, they fight for me
Revoking all the enemy's rights to my prosperity

My pen is mightier
and I've got an army
Marching up behind me
Warrior Women Wielding their Words
as Weapons of War

Every version of Me
Ready to stand up
Tear it up
Wreck shop and cut up
Step to the mic and put up
Never let up

Pen to paper
Write what the heart says now
Never wait til later
Passionate scribe pushing through pages
Molding together madlibs for the ages

My pen is mightier
My crown is heavier
My light shines brighter
Across every expanse and area

Touching hearts and tampering with souls
Kissing every inch of your earlobe
Cementing its way into your mind

My pen is mightier
And it only gets stronger with time
A full length story in every line
Can't nobody tell it like me
Cuz it's mine

I speak life and healing
I narrate every feeling
I tell of truth and transparency
All woven together like an imperfect tapestry

The woman I am today
Has come to save the girl I was yesterday
And I don't travel light
No matter when or where
the time is always right

To wield the pen as my sword
Cut through tension and silence
With all my might

Saying what needs to be said
Writing what needs to be read
Satisfying a soul that needs to be fed
Raising these dry bones from the dead

Opening the veil to life everlasting
Reaching out for everything worth grasping
Radically writing with rigorous recklessness
While Kanye shrugging

'Cuz it is what it is

My pen is mightier
Because I say it is!

Ode to My Oracle

Dance and make the Earth move.
Walk into a room and still everything.
Control the wind with your laugh.
Make the thunder rumble with your heart.
Goddess, be unchanged and unmoved.

Smile in the face of thine enemy.
Frown in the face of adversity, because they tried it!
Grow in spite of stifling influences.
Strength in your roots is unmatched.
Goddess, be unchanged and unmoved.

Sweet to the taste.
Strong to behold.
Bitterness knows not a place within you to find its home.
Love knows no existence without you breathing life into it.
Life has no meaning without you defining it.
Because, not all heroes wear capes.

So, hold the Earth in your hands
And the galaxies in your eyes.
Know your worth and then add according to your mood.
Queen Goddess, be unchanged.
Be unchained.
Be unmoved.
Be...

For T ♥

Super Dope-isms

#QuoteMe
"With every exhale, you breathe new life into me.
With every inhale, I breathe in the essence of you.
With every blink, I see you in a different light.
Every moment that ticks by is a lifetime
spent with you and even longer without you.
I have no explanation for any of it, but I enjoy it, nonetheless."

#QuoteMe
"Love is about freedom.
To love and be loved is a very freeing experience.
If you feel imprisoned or trapped
by your love for someone, you're not doing it right.
Make good choices. Choose FREEDOM."

#QuoteMe
"Love when you're unsure.
Love when you're scared.
Love like you never have before."

The Sculptured Man

When God created you
I am almost certain that his process
Went something like this...

Finding the rawest, purest clay
Deep, dark and charcoal-laced
He molded the foundation of you
No definition to behold but a vision all the same

He placed the basis of you upon the pedestal
Because he knew that you were meant to be revered
Drinking in the sight of you and what you would soon become
God caught a glimpse of His reflection and knew THAT was you

Molded from the essence of the earth
Features etched romantically into the raw clay
As God's great creation comes to life
The Sculptured Man...

Bronzed and beautiful
Boldly staring the Sun in its face
Embracing the tanning and toning his melanin was taking
Built from the ground up, towering above to be regaled

Measured movements making memorable markings
Bodacious brilliance built beautifully
Surgical scalpels scraping and shaping succinctly
The Sculptured Man...

Adonis and Anubis all in one
Warrior. God. Man of Magic and Mystery.
All touched, ordained, blessed and well-made
A masterpiece manipulated miraculously
The Sculptured Man...

God-like in his power and prowess
Prophet-like in his instruction
Warrior-like in his fierce ferocity
He is a lover who is loved
He is strength and sensitivity personified
He is wisdom and creativity, as I live and breathe

Beautifully, artfully, expertly made
The Sculptured Man...

Silence is Golden

The stillness of the night draws me closer
Wrapping its strong, dark presence around me
Holding me close...

The pitch-black ambiance relaxes me
The dancing shadows entertaining me
As I lie awake enveloped in the still of the night

The constant humming of my mind racing
The rhythmic melody of my own breathing
Singing me a sweet lullaby

That sneaky, sneaky moon...
How he creeps slowly across the expanse
Of my bedroom floor
Easing his soft light along the length of my bed
Until he comes to rest seductively upon my thighs

Lying in the embrace of the midnight hour
Singing to myself...

The Painted Lady

You can tell the Sun loved her
Just by looking at her
Only someone who loves you that much
Could kiss you that deeply
So deep, that it lived in her skin
Skin that glowed in the dark
And thrived in the light
Given by the one who loved her most

You can tell the Sun loved her
Just by looking at her
The Sun traced remnants of its love along her arms
Stroked its love intimately from her ankles to her belly button
Cupped her face in its hands and brushed kisses of love
Across her forehead, cheeks, nose, chin, eyes...

Rodan. Davinci. Picasso.
None of their strokes could match it
None of their passion showed more prominent
None of them loved nor created more beauty
With tender touches than the Sun

And you can tell the Sun loved her
Just by looking at her
Pouring itself on top of her like lava
Laying over her like the sweetest of lovers
Changing, molding, making the most passionate
Of love to every inch of her until she was completed

The masterpiece to behold
The manifestation of a solar sacrifice
Living proof of magic, wonder and more...
The Painted Lady...

Bronzed and bold
With a smile as bright as her beloved
Glistening in godliness
Glowing in greatness
The Painted Lady...

Brown and beautiful
Grace and femininity unmatched
With the strength of ten thousand men
And the softness of ten thousand bales of cotton
But just as heavy to carry, if ye be ill-prepared
To shoulder this Goddess
The Painted Lady...

Melanin melting off her like sweet chocolate
A Midas touch in her fingertips
Oceans and seas part beneath her feet
To give passage to this Queen
Ruler of moons, mountains, men and that sweet melanin

Melanin that embraces and caresses her
Like the Artist who made her
Because you can tell the Sun loved her
Just by the way he painted her

Cocoa kisses channeling cocoa blisses
Caramel caresses stroking her tresses
Vanilla-filled vacancies until every part is made whole

Leaving nothing to chance
No piece left untouched

Stroking. Touching. Shading. Brushing
Molding. Sculpting. Effecting. Adorning.
The Painted Lady...

You can tell the Sun loved her
Just by looking at her...

The Harmony of a Haiku #2

Your eyes are the Peace
Your hands are the Comfort
Your kiss is the Truth
Your heart is the Joy
The expanse of Passion
The Me & You

Black Love

My love for you is Black as fuck!
I'm talking shea butter back rubs
I'm talking Florida water in ya bathtub
I'm talking Granny's arms in a tight hug

I'm talking gospel music blasting early morning on a Saturday
No cartoons, just hymnal tunes allowed to play.
I'm talking plastic wrapped sofas in the room nobody's allowed in.
I'm talking that one old man
Granny keeps calling her "special friend."

I'm talking hot combs, rollers made of foam
and top of the ear burns on Easter morn.

I'm talking Malcom & Betty, Martin & 'Retta
I'm talking Ruby & Ossie, George & Weezie
That Black Love made perfect for TV.

My love for you is Black as fuck!
I'm talking afros with sunglasses and our fists up
I'm talking greased scalps smelling like coconut

I'm talking gold chains and bucket Kangols
I'm talking fingerwaves and cornrows
I'm talking Dwayne & Whitley,
back then he thought it was Kenu, but better he knew
I'm talking Uncle Phil and Aunt Viv,
you know which version we'll live

My love for you is Black as fuck!
Black like Nat & Harriet not giving a fuck
Black like 100-spoke rims on that big boy truck
Black like Hip Hop
Black like the King of Pop
Black like Rock & Roll
Black like the Queen of Soul
Black like Gospel and the Blues
Black like your mama telling you
not to play outside in your school shoes

My love for you is Black and deep
Like the expanse of the universe beyond where any eye can see
Fully unconquered, untapped and probably never will be.

Like Asé on the heels of an Amen
Like I am your woman and you are my man
Until this life ends and anew begins

Like praise dancers and four hour church services
Like Homecoming at Historically Black Colleges
Like a Second Line down a busy NOLA street
Like a cool glass of Georgia Sweet Tea
Like the spirit of our ancestors who refused to give up
My love for you is Black as fuck!

Entitled

I am a hopeless romantic
Held hostage in hook-up culture
Shackled by my sensitivity
and innate need for intimacy
No superheroes or first responders will come for me
I must escape this hell on my own...

I long for a love fully requited
Without pause or question
To be loved and adored with no hesitation
To be seen for who I am...
Fatally flawed and beautifully broken

To have my flaws and broken pieces handled with care
To show the darkest, grimiest parts of my soul to someone
Who's not afraid to get their hands dirty

To smile at the slightest thought
To blush at the sound of my name on your lips
To be shameless, blameless and free to be me

See, my list of demands is not long or overly complicated
For years, I allowed myself to believe
That I was asking too much
Demanding the damn-near impossible
So, my Stockholm set in and I became accustomed
to the less than bare minimum

Imprisoned...
Isolated...
Intolerable...
Instinct-ly abiding by scraps of what others felt I deserved

But, where my captors messed up...
Where they got the game fucked up...
Is that they allowed me enough time to become
Comfortable with my own company

Not being afraid to be alone
To find joy and comfort in my own compliments
Not leaning and depending on someone else to see
The DOPENESS that is Me!

Yeah, they done fucked up!

I found strength in my solitude
Power in my prison
And now I am unshackled, free to move
but, still barricaded away from bullshit
There's no room at the Inn for
Inconsistent Intimate Inmates

Meet my demands at the door
Or just meet the door
The choice is yours
but the final decision is mine

Accepting less than I deserve
While knowing I deserve it all
Is no longer an option

Sing my praises

Love me wholly without conditions
Earn me, dammit!
Do not entitle yourself to me or my love

You shall not pass
Or get this ass
Unless you prove worthy

No negotiator can speak for you
Because words ain't shit without matching actions
Ain't no Directors here to talk you through
All moves and motives are up to you

The time to put up or shut up has arrived
Hello? 9-1-1?
Meet my demands if you want everyone
To make it out alive!

Phinal Phaze

Vanilla-laced aromas fill the air around us
Heat and tension rising like a powder-keg ready to burst
You touch my hand...by accident, you claim...
Then you smile and blush slightly,
the faint hue decorating your face.

I laugh nervously, but never let go of your hand...
You look down...I look down...You look up...I look up...
Our eyes meet, my breath catches and time stands still...
Passion swirls in a thick purple haze...
As we slowly move through Step 1 of the final phase...

You graze my cheek with your knuckles in the softest way...
I remain shy, biting my lip...which only entices you...
You move closer to me, taking your time...easing my nerves...
I place my hand on your knee and you give in to the urge...

Slow touches...quick breaths...
Hormones raging...Slowly losing control...
Erotically emotional eyes lock in a gaze...
Two-stepping our way to the final phase...

I reach up...touching your lips with my delicate fingertips...
You kiss my palm ever-so gently, then push it to the side...
Like magnets, our lips touch...fusing together
2 seconds...3 seconds...
4 seconds...Forever...
You breathe...I breathe...Our lips meet...It gets better and better...

Our heartbeats play a symphony...
How sweet the sound...
Our bodies dance a seductive ballet...
Spinning this room 'round...
Skin searing from the slightest touch...
Eyes pitch black with the gloss of pure lust...

Falling fast into an ecstasy-filled haze...
In my temple, you may worship in the most sinful ways...
Dancing through the fiery flames of a sensual blaze...
Climbing higher and higher to this climactic final phase...

Talk That Talk

Kissing you is like a conversation
And I am hanging on your every word

Talk to me long
Talk to me nice
And don't be afraid
to say everything twice

Fluently flirting
with every inch of my lips
I won't need my passport
for this sensual trip

Speak to me with your native tongue
Teach me your language of love
Orgasmic-ly orating as you osculate against my orifice
Your perfect pout passionately pronouncing a palatable pledge
Endearing dialect in desirable diction
making a delectable declaration

Stake your claim on my attention
Capture my breath as your willing prisoner
Tantalizingly tracing temptation with the tip of your tongue
Lyrically lacing our lips together with every lick

Puckering and petting without pause
Pillow-talk to me without words
Whisper sweet nothings against my lips

Breathless and yearning from our formulated foreplay

Kissing you is like a conversation
And I could talk to you all day

Super Dope-isms

#QuoteMe
_"Empty Apologies are fabrications of false emotions
used for the purposes of pacifying the offended, and I am not a fan."_

#QuoteMe
_"The "S" on my chest stands for Sensitive and I wear it proudly.
Like a badge of honor or a Warrior's shield.
It is the core of who I am
and I refuse to be shamed by it any longer."_

#QuoteMe
_"Sometimes our incessant need to be the hero
leads you to drown in someone else's pool of poison."
~ Pastor Sarah Jakes-Roberts ~_

The Disclaimer

Listen! I got some shit to say to you niggas
Out here getting beside yourselves
See, you think you slick!
Slipping and sliding through DMs and inboxes
like you Shaunie Davis or some shit

Check it out though...

That cute shit you wrote to her?
Her friends already know
That freaky shit you said to her?
Her friends already know

That one date you took her on?
Opening doors, pulling out chairs, paying for movie tickets,
letting her get extra butter on her popcorn and shit
Guess what...
Her friends already know!

Dudes these days underestimate
the powerful bond of female friendships
Being your Sister's Keeper is a job that women do proudly
Thinking you can hold her hand
While whispering sweet nothings in her home girl's ear?

Congratulations, you played ya'self!

But, I get why you tried it.

We've been slacking on mending and maintaining
the bond between Sistas
We give in to the temptations of drama and deceit,
bitching about betrayal and catty confusion
And for what?

Some piece of a man who told you how thick you were
For that fool who said "You look way better than your friend"
Or that idiot who stood on his soapbox to rant about how
women with natural hair are better than those who wear weaves
And on Tuesdays, he makes that same argument in reverse

Fucking clowns!

These bum-fuckboys who figured out what an opinion was
and now you can't shut them up
These masters of reverse psychology who can convince you
that the same woman who let you borrow her favorite heels
or cry on her couch while you inhaled her favorite wine
is "Not really your friend"

We as women have made it so easy for them
To get inside our heads because we've led them to believe
That the control lies between our legs
And sadly, we started to believe it too
Aye, Sis! Cut that shit out!

Love your sister from another mister
Cherish that Queen who is the Thelma to your Louise
And the Blanche to your Rose

Stop giving these niggas access to the Queendom
you two built with your own blood, sweat and tears
while rocking spray-painted tees that said "Best Friends 4eva!"

Check that goof-troop at the door
Throw down your blanket of spike strips,
flattening the tires on his rolling tank of bullshit
as he tries to ghost ride the whip through your DMs

Take your Sistas hand in yours,
look that nigga square in the face and sing:
"My friends and I share a lot of things. Dick ain't one of them!"

Super Dope-isms

<u>**#QuoteMe**</u>
"Have you ever wished for an endless night?
Lassoed the moon and the stars and pulled that rope tight?
Have you ever held your breath and asked yourself,
will you ever get better than tonight?"
<u>*~Glitter in the Air* by Pink~</u>

<u>**#QuoteMe**</u>
"You are not broken.
You are just a beautiful work of art in progress."

<u>**#QuoteMe**</u>
"The life you live writes the Love Story you'll have."

<u>**#QuoteMe**</u>
"In the midst of the madness is where you grow the most."

Jigsaw

I want to press our broken selves together tightly until
all our jagged pieces mold into a masterful mosaic of matrimony...
Let the grime of my truth cover your hands like the finest gloves...
Wear it proudly and do not be afraid...

Let me decorate the damaged parts of you
with the Gold trimmings of my adoration for you...
Let me love the lonely out of you
while you light up the darkness in me....

Bound by our bad experiences...
Trauma tying us together in kindred knots...
Drawn nearer by never-ending desire...
Shackled soul-to-soul for a sleepless lifetime...

You are mine.
I am yours.
This love is ours.
This story is ours.
The chapters of You & Me
melded together into the Saga of We...

Etching an eternity into Heaven & Earth...
Spiritually seductive scriptures
scribed more soulful than Solomon's symphony...
Music of my heart...
Muse of my life...

A love untapped and unknown at heights unreachable...
I'd climb forever just to fall for you on purpose for always...

Mirror, Mirror

Show me the ugliest parts of you
and I'll show you why you're beautiful.

I'll love the worst parts of you the most,
just so you can learn to love them at all.

Let me show you what it feels like to be loved
and appreciated as your WHOLE self,
not just the good parts.

The invaluable worthiness of you,
is a price far above rubies.

Diamonds reflect the beauty within,
like clam shells part to showcase its pearls.

The golden hue of your soul,
bursts through like the early morning sun.
Bringing forth beauty and newness with every flicker.

You are the joy long sought for and prayed about.
You are the dawning patiently waited for.
You are the gift that is never-ending.
You are the priceless treasure now found,
that was once buried and forgotten.

For every time you forget,
I shall remind you.

For every ounce of reassurance you need,
I will provide it for you.

Compliments given and praises sung
at the highest of octaves.
Full tank, gassing you up
with the highest quality octane.
The only voice louder than your own,
will be mine reaffirming every glorious thing you are.

No matter what it is or who you used to be,
show me the ugliest parts of you,
so I can show you why you're beautiful, anyway.

The Benediction

Dear God,

Thank you for second chances...

For lifetimes, I have pridefully rambled on about how I don't give second chances and I don't go backwards in relationships...once ties are cut, that's it. My actions were often very selfish and self-serving, giving no consideration to the other parties involved. My sole focus was my feelings and disappointments.

I absorbed and internalized everything, making it about me in the most negative ways possible. I would then become so consumed by my anger, grief and other emotions...leaving no room for forgiveness and reconciliations with people.

However, I've realized there have been many times where you softened my heart and dropped my barriers to let certain people back into my life, especially in a time when I really needed them specifically. I am grateful to you for taking the reins in situations where I thought I had things under control. Those were the times I needed you most.

Thank you for giving me infinite second chances and redo's in this life. Thank you for bringing me to and through situations, showing me the importance of time and valuing and mending relationships. Thank you for a sense of responsibility and good intentions.

Thank you for my stubborn but forgiving heart, in spite of how much I might fight it. Amen!

"Authenticity unlocks God's ability." ---Pastor Sarah Jakes-Roberts

Author Bio

ShaRhonda is originally from Maywood, IL, and currently resides in Atlanta, GA. She is a self-proclaimed "Writer-by-Passion, not by-trade," and has been published numerous times across various publications, including a collection of self-published works.

She holds a Master of Written Communications degree from National Louis University in Chicago and currently works in the Telecommunications field as a means to fund the dream of being a highly paid, best-selling author someday.

In between her many passion projects, she moonlights as a freelance content writer, copy editor and blogger.

Continue to follow her writing journey: